Mysterious Encounters

Unicorns

by Elizabeth Silverthorne

KIDHAVEN PRESS

An imprint of Thomson Gale, a part of The Thomson Corporation

THOMSON

™

GALE

Detroit • New York • San Francisco • New Haven, Conn. • Waterville, Maine • London

© 2008 Thomson Gale, a part of The Thomson Corporation.

Thomson and Star Logo are trademarks and Gale and KidHaven Press are registered trademarks used herein under license.

For more information, contact
KidHaven Press
27500 Drake Rd.
Farmington Hills, MI 48331-3535
Or you can visit our Internet site at http://www.gale.com

Picture Credits

Cover photo: © Francis G. Mayer/CORBIS; © Alinari Archives/Corbis, 37; The Art Archive/Cathédrale de Notre Dame Reims/Dagli Orti, 38; The Art Archive/Galleria Borghese Rome/Dagli Orti, 36; Ken Bohn/Zoological Society of San Diego via Getty Images, 34; The Bridgeman Art Library/Getty Images, 19; © Christie's Images/Corbis, 24; © Corbis, 12; Richard Ellis/Photo Researchers, Inc., 30; Flemish School/The Bridgeman Art Library/Getty Images, 18; French School/The Bridgeman Art Library/Getty Images, 40; Yann Layma/The Image Bank/Getty Images, 10; The Library of Congress, 16; © Mary Evans Picture Library/Edwin Wallace/The Image Works, 21; © Mary Evans Picture Library/The Image Works, 7; © Buddy Mays/Corbis, 6, 27; © Werner Forman Archive/Topham/The Image Works, 9

LIBRARY OF CONGRESS CATALOGING-IN-PUBLICATION DATA

Silverthorne, Elizabeth, 1930–
  Unicorns / by Elizabeth Silverthorne.
    p. cm. — (Mysterious encounters)
  Includes bibliographical references and index.
  ISBN-13: 978-0-7377-3782-0 (hardcover)
  1. Unicorns. I. Title.
  GR830.U6S55 2008
  398.24'54—dc22

                                                        2007022223

ISBN-10: 0-7377-3782-4

Printed in the United States of America

Contents

Chapter 1

The First Unicorns

Long before people learned to read and write, they believed in unicorns. Of all the tales of fabulous beasts, those about unicorns are the oldest. Reports of sightings of other mysterious animals such as werewolves, vampires, Bigfoot, and the Loch Ness Monster created a sense of dread and fear. But tales of unicorn sightings almost always created a sense of delight and awe.

What Is a Unicorn?

Today, the name "unicorn" usually brings to mind an image of a graceful, white horselike creature with a spiraled horn growing out of its forehead. Through the centuries, however, in different countries there have been very different accounts of what unicorns looked like and how they behaved.

Some unicorns were huge; others were tiny. Some bellowed like bulls; others had voices like musical chimes. A few were fierce, but most were gentle. Some were multicolored, and some were silver or pure white. The two constants in all the descriptions were that the creature had a single horn growing out of its head and that it had magical powers. Since no one has ever proven the existence of unicorns, it is all the more curious that these two details appear in unicorn descriptions from different countries through the centuries. In *The Lore of the Unicorn*, unicorn expert Odell Shepard says: "We may never know precisely when or where or how the legend of the unicorn began."[1]

The Mysterious Unicorn

When and where people first got the idea of a creature such as a unicorn is a mystery. Whether this idea was based on any living animal is also a mystery. But the greatest mystery is: Why has the unicorn fascinated people in almost every corner of the world for so many centuries?

Most people think of a unicorn as a majestic, horselike creature with a spiraled horn.

The Unicorn in the Sky

Although its origins are lost, one interesting myth persisted in the Far East. Primitive people wondered why the Moon seemed to follow the Sun across the sky. They decided the Sun and the Moon represented the beasts they called the lion and the unicorn. Each month the unicorn (the New Moon) chased the lion (the Sun) across the sky. The New Moon's sharp tip resembled the horn of the unicorn, and the Sun was anxious to keep out of its way. But when the Moon became round and fat, the Sun devoured it. After a brief disappearance, the Moon/unicorn was reborn as a slender crescent, and the chase began again. During a solar eclipse, when the Sun was hidden behind the Moon, they thought it was the Sun/lion that briefly died. Some of the stories told by these early people connected unicorns not only with the sky, but also with the creation of the Earth.

The Gentle Ki-lin

According to an ancient Chinese myth, the creator of the world was assisted by four sacred beasts: the dragon, the **phoenix**, the tortoise, and the unicorn. The Chinese unicorn (called *Ki-lin* and pronounced

In one ancient story the Sun and Moon represent a lion and a unicorn chasing each other across the sky.

The Unicorn in the Milky Way

Many constellations visible in the night sky have been named after fanciful beasts. According to this custom, a fairly new discovery (from the 17th century) is called the Unicorn Constellation (Monoceros). It is a dim cluster of stars in the winter Milky Way, but it can be seen clearly with a telescope.

"chee-lin") was a symbol of good luck, revered for its wisdom and goodness. Although descriptions differed, traditionally it was said to have a brightly-colored body covered with scales, a voice like a thousand chimes, and a very long horn. It avoided fighting, refused to eat any living creature, and walked so softly it did not crush the blades of grass under its feet. The Ki-lin was given credit for helping humans in many ways.

The earliest reported appearance of a Ki-lin was to a legendary emperor, Fu Hsi. He is said to have ruled China about 5,000 years ago, before there was writing. One day Fu Hsi was walking along the Yellow River thinking how sad it was that people's thoughts died when they did. Suddenly out of the river a miraculous creature arose. James Cross Giblin describes this unicorn in *The Truth About Unicorns:* "It had the body of a deer, the tail of an ox, the head of a wolf, and the hooves of a horse. Out of its forehead grew a single horn, several feet long. And tied to its back was a large, rolled package."[2]

Kneeling before the emperor, the unicorn turned its head, pointing to the package with its horn. When the emperor opened it he found a large roll of paper. From the markings on this paper

The Chinese unicorn, the Ki-lin, is described as having many-colored scales, a long horn, and a musical voice.

he was able to create a written language for his people.

The Unicorn and Confucius

The Ki-lin was said to appear when a great leader was about to be born or about to die. The most famous appearance of this kind was to the mother-to-be of Confucius (551?–479 B.C.). According to legend, his mother was traveling to a shrine to pray for a son. A Ki-lin appeared and knelt before her. It dropped a tablet of jade into her outstretched hand. On the tablet was a poem praising the son she would have. When Confucius grew up, he became known for his wisdom and lived up to everything the poem said about him. The Ki-lin appeared

A Ki-lin predicted that Confucius (pictured) would grow up to be a great leader.

again shortly before Confucius died. When Confucius heard that hunters had killed the unicorn, he said that he had lost his Tao (his way or path) and refused to write anymore.

The Unicorn Man

The unicorn of India was not a beast at all—it was a handsome young man! His name was Risharinga, which means antelope horn. His story is told in the *Mahabharata*, a famous record of Indian history and myths. Like other stories in this collection, the story of the unicorn man was told and retold for hundreds of years before it was written down.

Risharinga's parents were a Hindu holy man and a beautiful doe antelope (actually a young maiden transformed into a doe by evil spirits). Their baby boy was like other humans in every way, except he had a single curved horn growing out of his forehead. When he grew up, he fell in love with the king's daughter. She loved him, too, but the king objected to her marrying this strange-looking young man.

India was in a terrible condition because of a severe drought. For a very long time there had been no rain. However, when the unicorn man wept tears of sorrow for the misery of the farmers and for the dying animals, the rain began to fall. Then the grateful king gave his daughter to the gentle man who had saved the land through his pity and compassion. This fairy tale ends with the princess and the unicorn man marrying and living happily ever after.

Other Eastern Unicorns

The Japanese unicorn (the *sin-you*) had a mane like a lion. It was supposed to know right from wrong and was called on to judge people accused of wrongdoing. If it found a person to be guilty, it fixed its eerie gaze on the criminal and pierced him through the heart with its horn.

In Persia (what is today called Iran) the unicorn was called the *Karkadann*. Of all the different accounts of ancient unicorns it was by far the fiercest. It was as large as a rhinoceros with a tail like a lion. Each of its legs had three hooves. A curved black horn rose from its forehead. The Karkadann had a voice so deep and powerful that when it bellowed, other animals fled in terror. The Earth shook when it ran. Even this fierce unicorn, however, had its soft side. When it drank the morning dew from green plants, it behaved calmly. The only

A sculpture from ancient Persia shows a procession of unicorns (above) and lions (below).

creature that could tame it was the dove. When it heard the dove's gentle voice, it would lie down beneath the tree where the bird nested and wait for the dove to alight on its horn.

The Unicorn in the West

Three centuries before the birth of Christ, historians in Western countries began mentioning stories they had heard of Eastern unicorns. Different writers and artists in countries of the Western world created different notions of how unicorns looked and what they did, and unicorn lore grew tremendously. In addition to being described as a mysterious, elusive beast with magical abilities and a single horn, the unicorn became a symbol of many different ideas.

Chapter 2

Unicorn Tales

Travelers' tales of unicorns in the Far East grabbed the attention of listeners in other countries. It seemed possible—even probable—that such a creature might exist. People really *wanted* such a fabulous animal to exist. And for centuries they believed that it did.

The First Written Record

The first widely read accounts of unicorn sightings were written by a Greek physician named Ctesias (pronounced "**tee**-see-us") about 2,500 years ago. While visiting in Persia, Ctesias listened to the tales of the traders in the bazaars. Along with their goods they brought back stories of life in the East.

Readers were especially impressed with his description of unicorns:

There are in India certain wild asses which are as large as horses, and larger. Their bodies are white, their heads dark red, and their eyes dark blue. They have a horn on the forehead which is about a foot-and-a-half in length. The base of the horn is pure white; the upper part is sharp and a vivid crimson; and the remainder, or middle portion, is black. . . . The animal is exceedingly swift and powerful, so that no creature, neither the horse nor any other, can overtake it.[3]

As a physician, Ctesias was impressed by accounts of the medicinal powers of the unicorn's horn. He

The Dinosaur Unicorn

In the American Museum of Natural History in New York City is a fossil skeleton of a real dinosaur unicorn. It was a large, plant-eating animal that roamed in northern Asia and North America in the Cretaceous period, about 120 million years ago. Its scientific name is *Monoclonius nasicornus.* The Monoclonius had one horn growing out of its nose.

said that powder filed from the horn could be mixed with a liquid and drunk as a protection against poison. He also noted that a person who drank wine from one of the horns would never suffer from convulsions.

The Reports Spread

Other writers in Greece and Rome picked up Ctesias's description of unicorns and added to it. Some told of different unicorns seen in remote parts of the world. One of the most famous figures of the ancient world added to the lore with a firsthand account. In his *Gallic Wars*, Julius Caesar (100–44 B.C.) described a unicorn that lived in an enormous forest in

Julius Caesar (pictured) claimed to have seen a unicorn while he was traveling in Germany.

Germany: "A huge beast with the form of a stag, from the middle of whose brow and between the ears there stood forth one horn, longer and straighter than the horns known to the Romans."[4]

Many of the accounts of unicorns around the first century A.D. were gathered from stories told by other writers and from hearsay accounts by traders and travelers. As Christianity began to spread, references to unicorns in the Bible greatly increased interest in the legendary creature.

Unicorns in the Bible

There are seven clear references to the unicorn in the Old Testament of the King James Version of the Bible. In Numbers 23:22, for example, it says: "He [God] hath as it were the strength of the unicorn." Later versions of the Bible changed the references from "unicorn" to "wild ox." Biblical scholars are still struggling with the problem of which animal was meant. But as Odell Shepard points out, each of the seven allusions is consistent in "bringing before us a beast remarkable for strength, ferocity, wildness, and unconquerable spirit."[5]

In the book of Genesis, Adam was given the task of naming all the animals. In some translations, the unicorn was the first animal he named. When God heard this, he reached down and touched its horn. From that time on it was first among all the beasts. It was also the one animal that accompanied Adam and Eve when they were forced to leave the Garden of Eden.

One folktale relates a story about how unicorns were too big to fit in Noah's Ark.

There are several humorous folktales about the animals that boarded Noah's ark. In one of them the unicorn is mentioned as being too big and taking up too much room to fit on the ark. In another tale it is too demanding and so is thrown off the boat by Noah. When Noah changes his mind and tries to persuade the unicorn to come aboard, it refuses. Then, during the forty days and nights of the Flood, the unicorn stays afloat by swimming in circles around the ark.

Genghis Khan Meets a Unicorn

A more serious legend of a unicorn encounter is connected with the history of India. In the 13th century Genghis Khan, a Mongolian warrior, had ambitions to conquer the whole known world. He succeeded in conquering much of Asia and built a huge empire. Khan was very close to his father. After his father died, Khan asked his father's spirit for guidance before each battle.

By 1224 Khan's army was on the march toward India. It rolled on ruthlessly, conquering town after town and climbing mountain after mountain. Finally Khan and his soldiers reached the last mountain and were ready to sweep down and capture India. Before sunrise Khan climbed to the top of the mountain to plan the battle. To his surprise a strange beast stepped from behind a large boulder. Writer Kevin Owens describes it: "It was small, about the size of a young deer, green, and it had a single horn of red and black protruding from its forehead."[6] Khan recognized it as the Ki-lin, the unicorn of which he had heard many tales.

He watched in amazement as the unicorn fixed its eyes on him and knelt three times at his feet. He felt that his father was looking at him through the eyes of the unicorn. He thought his father's spirit was warning him not to go on. Shouting to his warriors, who had gathered ready for battle, Khan told them to turn back. The unicorn disappeared, but it had saved India from invasion.

Genghis Khan is said to have seen a unicorn on a mountaintop in India.

Bestiaries

A bestiary was a book about beasts, real and imaginary. A mixture of fact and fiction, they were immensely popular in the Middle Ages. A 9th-century bestiary published in Switzerland described the unicorn as a small animal, like a young goat, with a sharp horn. It was, the author reported, a fierce fighter that could be captured only when it was tricked into laying its head in the lap of a young maiden.

Alexander and the Unicorn

Alexander the Great (356–323 B.C.) was another warrior who set out to be a world conqueror. He, too, was a real person with a real place in history. Because he accomplished amazing feats, legends about him grew until truth and myth were tangled. One of the enduring stories is that his famous steed, Bucephalus, was a unicorn. It was said to have the body of a horse and the head of an ox.

According to this story a unicorn had been captured and presented to Alexander's father, King Philip of Macedonia. The wild creature fiercely resisted all attempts to ride it. Philip's champion riders tried and failed to tame it. The beast was about to be taken away as useless. Alexander, who was only thirteen, asked permission to try to tame it. His father agreed, but laid out conditions. If Alexander failed, he would have to pay the cost of the creature. If he succeeded, the unicorn would be his to keep. Instead of trying to leap onto its back and control the unicorn by force, Alexander spoke to it softly. He stroked it and leaned against it so it could feel

Some accounts say that Alexander the Great's beloved horse, Bucephalus, was really a unicorn.

the weight of his body. When the creature became calm, Alexander mounted it and rode off.

Alexander rode Bucephalus into every major battle during his conquest of Egypt and the Persian Empire. Bucephalus died during Alexander's last great battle in India. With his death Alexander's fortunes and extraordinary luck changed. He died at the young age of thirty-two. Many believed that Bucephalus was a horse, but many others insisted he was a unicorn.

The Desire to Believe

Numerous tales exist of less famous adventurers who encountered unicorns. If there were such strange-looking animals as giraffes and hippopotamuses, people reasoned, why couldn't there be unicorns? In the Middle Ages in Europe, stories of the wonderful powers of the unicorn's horn added greatly to the desire to believe there was such a creature.

Chapter 3

The Magical Horn

Just as early descriptions of unicorns varied wildly, so did descriptions of their horns. They might be from a foot (.30m) to 12 feet (3.66m) long. They might be white, black, silver, gold, or two or three different colors. They might be spiraled or smooth, fixed or moveable. People in the Middle Ages called the unicorn's horn an alicorn. The most important thing about the alicorn, they believed, was its power to cure and prevent diseases.

The Alicorn as Medicine

The Greek physician Ctesias insisted that his description of unicorns came from reliable witnesses.

An artist depicts people dying from the plague in the 1300s. Alicorn was said to cure the plague.

He was also convinced that stories of the wonderful power of the horn to cure ailments were true. Other reputable writers spread stories of the medicinal powers of the alicorn, until it became as common a belief as the belief in witches. It was prescribed as a cure for everything from the **plague** and mad dog bites to loss of memory and aging.

Alicorn was listed as an approved medicine in official lists published by the Royal Society of Physicians in London as late as 1740. People bought alicorn from pharmacists in the form of powder to treat such ailments as stomach aches. Even a tiny bit of alicorn was very expensive.

The Alicorn as Protection

In medieval times, people in Europe who had high positions and great wealth lived in constant fear of being poisoned. Poisoning was a convenient way of removing rivals or enemies. As tales of the power of alicorn to detect poison became widespread, there was a huge demand for it.

Alicorns were used in a variety of ways to reveal poison. Sometimes one was set in the middle of a dining table. If any of the dishes contained poison, it was believed the horn would begin to sweat. Eating utensils themselves—goblets, cups, and bowls—were made of alicorn. It was thought that even a small piece of alicorn was effective. According to this

The Whole Animal as Medicine

In the 12th century Saint Hildegarde of Germany was well known for her medical writings. She wrote that an ointment made of powdered unicorn's liver mixed with egg yolks could cure leprosy. She also said that a belt made of unicorn's skin kept one from having the plague. And she advised wearing unicorn leather boots to assure healthy feet, thighs, and joints.

belief, a nobleman might have a tiny piece of horn attached to a silver chain. A servant dipped it into his master's wine glass each time it was refilled. If the wine frothed, that was a sign it contained poison.

A Costly Treasure

Although alicorn was rare and costly, many royals, nobles, and high churchmen yearned to possess one of these precious objects. Not only was it considered an effective detector of poison, it was also a symbol of high status. James Giblin says,

> The Holy Roman Emperor Charles V, who ruled between 1519 and 1556, gave a German noble two horns as payment for a debt equal to a million dollars in today's money. When Queen Elizabeth I came to the throne of England in 1558, an inventory was taken of the royal treasury. Its one unicorn horn was valued at 10,000 pounds. In Elizabeth's day, that amount would buy a large country estate with a castle on it.[7]

King Frederick III, ruler of Denmark from 1648 to 1670, had a throne built of alicorns. Those who saw it considered it a wonder, and many compared it to the ivory and gold throne of King Solomon mentioned in the Bible.

Alicorn as Purifier

Belief in the powers of the alicorn continued to grow. It was said to cure almost every known disease, including the dreaded plague. It could detect the smallest amount of poison in food or drink. It made the air around it pure. It also (while attached to the unicorn) could clear large bodies of water.

According to legend, the unicorn purified water for the benefit of other animals. A Greek **bestiary** written between the 12th and 14th centuries includes this tale:

> There is a stream where the animals gather to drink. But before they have assembled, the serpent comes and casts its poison into the water. The animals mark well the poison and do not dare to drink and they wait for the unicorn. He comes and immediately goes into the stream and, dipping his horn in the water, renders the poison harmless. Then he drinks, and all of the other animals drink as well.[8]

According to legend, the unicorn could use its horn to purify water.

A priest who claimed to have been an eyewitness also described this performance. In 1389 John of Hesse, a priest from Holland, visited the Holy Land. He described a trip to the River Marah, which he said had "very bitter" water. "Venomous animals poison that water after the setting of the sun," he wrote, "so that the good animals cannot drink of it; but in the morning, after the sunrise, comes the unicorn and dips his horn into the stream, driving the poison from it so that the good animals can drink there during the day. This I have seen myself."[9]

The Sea Unicorn

When something is extremely valuable and very scarce, dishonest people try to profit from it. So crooked merchants sometimes tried to substitute bones of pigs, dogs, and goats for "real" alicorns. But what was a "real" alicorn? There were some tales of unicorn hunts. But there was no evidence that unicorns were being captured or killed in large enough numbers to meet the demand for their horns. Where, then, did the precious alicorns actually come from?

The answer is that they came from whales. Danish seamen had prized (and sold) the single long tusk of an unusual marine creature since at least the 12th century. They called it a *narhval* (**narwhal** in English). Even though they were buying narwhal tusks as alicorns, most Europeans were not aware

Testing for Fake Alicorn

Elaborate tests were used to distinguish "real" alicorn from fake alicorn. One of these was to place spiders in a ring drawn on the floor using a piece of horn. If the horn was genuine, the spiders could not cross the ring. Another test was to place the horn in cold water. If the water bubbled but remained cold, the alicorn was thought to be real.

that such a creature existed until 1577. This was the year a British sea captain, Martin Frobisher, announced an amazing discovery: In the icy seas above Greenland, he had found a sea unicorn!

It was round, he said, like a porpoise and about 12 feet (3.66m) long. Its most unusual feature was its hollow, spiraled horn, which was about half the length of its body. He had tested it, he claimed, and believed it to be a true alicorn. When he returned to England, he proudly presented it to Queen Elizabeth I. It was given a prominent place in the royal treasury along with the other alicorn she had inherited.

Drawings showing narwhals with horns growing out of their foreheads circulated. There was a widespread belief that a sea creature existed to match every land creature, and for the many who believed in land unicorns, a sea unicorn seemed entirely possible. The trade in alicorns continued to flourish for many years. There were, however, beginning to be some who challenged their powers.

The Alicorn in Doubt

Scientists who examined the "horn" of the narwhal began to point out that it grew from the jaw, not from the forehead. In 1621, the pioneer geographer Gerhardus Mercator wrote, "Among the fish of Iceland is included the narwhal. It has a tooth in its head which projects to a length of as much as 10 feet [3.05m]. Some sell this tooth as a unicorn's horn."[10]

In 1638, Ole Worm, a Danish physician, stated flatly that the narwhal's horn was not a horn at all,

The narwhal, with its long tusk, has been mistakenly described as a unicorn.

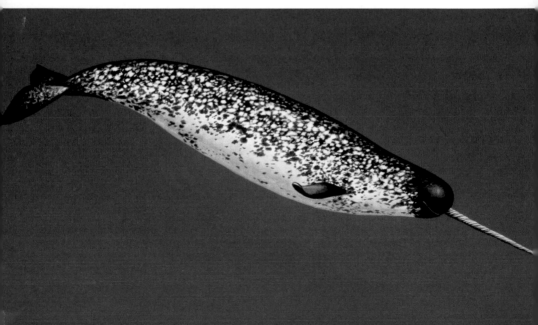

A Doubter

Apollonius, a Greek writer in the 1st century A.D., traveled to India, where he saw the one-horned creatures called unicorns. But when he heard that the rulers of the country drank from unicorn horn cups to protect themselves against sickness, he said he would have believed it if the kings had been immortal!

but a tooth or tusk. Worm had his own museum in Copenhagen. On exhibit there were a narwhal's skull and tusk. Despite this evidence, however, many Danes and other Europeans continued to believe in the sea unicorn.

Chapter 4

Hunting the Unicorn

Belief in unicorns and their magical powers was hard to shake. Before the 20th century, medicine was a very inexact science. Often it was mixed with magic. If alicorn could cure and protect, people wanted more than ever to believe there were unicorns. Another reason for accepting the existence of unicorns was that they became identified with Jesus Christ. The church had immense influence in the Middle Ages. If it accepted unicorns as symbols of Jesus, few would deny they existed. And so the hunt continued.

Marco Polo

Marco Polo (1254?–1324) was one of the first explorers to mention unicorns. After a visit to Suma-

The Lion and the Unicorn

The tradition that the lion and the unicorn hate each other goes back thousands of years. Before England (the lion) and Scotland (the unicorn) were united, a popular nursery rhyme said:

> The lion and the unicorn
> Were fighting for the crown;
> The lion chased the unicorn
> All around the town.

When England and Scotland united in 1603 the lion and the unicorn became a part of the British royal coat of arms.

Quoted in James Cross Giblin, *The Truth About Unicorns.* New York: HarperCollins, 1991, p. 81.

tra, a large island in Southeast Asia, he described the strange "unicorns" he had seen:

They have wild elephants, and great numbers of unicorns hardly smaller than elephants in size. Their hair is like that of a buffalo, and their feet like those of an elephant. In the middle of their forehead is a very large black horn. Their head is like that of a wild boar, and is always carried bent to the ground. They delight in living in mire and mud. It is a hideous beast to look at, and in no way like what we think and say in our countries, namely a beast that lets itself be taken in the lap of a virgin. Indeed, I assure you it is altogether different from what we fancied.[11]

What Polo had seen was the one-horned rhinoceros. His disappointment in this ugly, muddy "unicorn" reveals two things. First, it shows that Europeans pictured unicorns as the attractive creatures Polo had expected them to be. Second, it reveals the common belief that a unicorn could be captured only when a young maiden lured it into laying its head in her lap.

Marco Polo mistook a rhinoceros for a unicorn while traveling on the island of Sumatra.

The Unicorns of Ethiopia

Prester John (Priest John) was a legendary ruler who was supposed to have lived in the 1100s. Explorers from Spain and Portugal reported that he was the emperor of Ethiopia. They said they had seen many unicorns among the animals at his fabulous court. Travelers in the time of Elizabeth I reported that these unicorns (or their descendants) still existed at the former court of Prester John.

Edward Webbe, an Elizabethan adventurer, wrote, "I have seen in a place like a park adjoyning unto prester John's Court, three score and seventeene unicornes and eliphants all alive at one time, and they were so tame that I have played with them as one would play with young Lambes."[12]

Jeronimo Lobo (1593–1678), a missionary to Ethiopia, reported that he had seen the unicorn there. He said:

> The prodigious Swiftness with which this Creature runs from one Wood into another has given me no Opportunity of examining it particularly, yet I have had so near a sight of it as to be able to give some Description of it. The Shape is the same as that of a beautiful Horse, exact and nicely proportion'd of a Bay Colour, with a black Tail, which in some Provinces is long, in others very short; some have long Manes hanging to the Ground.[13]

One adventurer described a park in Ethiopia filled with unicorns, elephants, and other creatures.

The German Einhorn

German-speaking people were strong believers in unicorns. They called them einhorns. Images of einhorns filled German palaces and churches during the Middle Ages, and they called the Virgin Mary "Maria Unicornis" (Mary of the Unicorn).

Einhorns were thought to live in the Harz Mountains region of central Germany. There is an enduring legend of how a unicorn saved an old wise woman who lived in a cave in this area. People came from far away to ask her for medicines and advice. But the church denounced her as a witch. A monk was sent with soldiers to arrest her. As they climbed up to the cave, a pale unicorn stepped out of the forest. It went up to the woman and knelt before her. She got up on its back and rode away. Then the story says:

> The monk and soldiers ran after her, but the soldiers soon fell behind because of their heavy armor and weapons. The monk was finally able to catch up with the woman, but as he tried to grab her, she raised her arms and made signs in the air and disappeared. By the time the soldiers reached the spot, all they found was a hole in the ground with the monk lying shattered and lifeless at the bottom. The soldiers buried the monk and named the cave Einhornhohle—a name it has been known by ever since.[14]

The German einhorn was said to have rescued a woman who was suspected of witchcraft.

Unicorns in the New World

Sightings of unicorns were also reported in America. In the 16th century, two reports of unicorns in Florida circulated. In the 17th century, Dr. Olfert Dapper described unicorn sightings in Maine and on the Canadian border. "On the Canadian border," he said, "there are sometimes seen animals resembling horses, but with cloven hoofs, rough manes, a long straight horn upon the forehead, a curled tail

A tapestry from the 1500s depicts a unicorn with a long, straight horn.

The "Living Unicorn"

In 1985, Ringling Brothers Circus announced it had a great new attraction: a "living unicorn." The unicorn entered the arena on a gold float accompanied by a young woman in a glittering costume. The circus actually had four unicorn pretenders—goats with horns grown from transplanted horn buds of a bull calf. But protests by animal rights activists soon ended the performances.

like that of the wild boar, black eyes, and a neck like that of a stag. They live in the loneliest wilderness."[15]

In the early years of the 20th century, belief and interest in unicorn legends seemed to be fading. Then in 1933 a Maine doctor, Franklin Dove, turned a bull calf into a unicorn by manipulating the animal's horn buds to create a single horn. James Giblin says, "The horn emerged thick and straight, and the unicorn bull seemed perfectly content with it. He used it to pass under fences by raising the bottom wire and to defend himself against other animals. But he almost never used the horn to attack another creature. Like his namesake, Dove's unicorn bull turned out to be a gentle beast."[16]

A tapestry depicts the ancient legend of a wild unicorn being tamed by a maiden.

The Imaginary Unicorn

In the 1930s, while Dove was attempting to create a live unicorn, the unicorn of the imagination had a rebirth. In 1938 the magnificent **Unicorn Tapestries** went on display in the Cloisters Museum in New York City. No one knows exactly when or where they were made. The seven richly colored panels have a special room in the museum. They tell a simple story. A band of hunters track a beautiful white unicorn. A young maiden tames it. The hunters kill it and bring its dead body back to a castle. In the last tapestry, the unicorn miraculously returns to life.

Each year thousands of people stand and gaze at the creature pictured in the tapestries. This is the image they will probably think of afterward when they think of a unicorn: a noble, horselike creature with a creamy coat, a curly beard, a plumed tail, and a long, spiraled horn. It is a creature that may be captured by cunning, but its spirit can never be conquered. Just as it has for untold centuries, the image of the proud unicorn still has the power to inspire.

Notes

Chapter 1: The First Unicorns

1. Odell Shepard, *The Lore of the Unicorn*. New York: Harper & Row, 1979, p. 25.
2. James Cross Giblin, *The Truth About Unicorns*. New York: HarperCollins, 1991, pp. 23–24.

Chapter 2: Unicorn Tales

3. Quoted in Giblin, *The Truth About Unicorns*, p. 8.
4. Quoted in Shepard, *The Lore of the Unicorn*, p. 40.
5. Shepard, *The Lore of the Unicorn*, p. 42.
6. Kevin Owens, "Genghis Khan," All about Unicorns. www.allaboutunicorns.com/warriors.php.

Chapter 3: The Magical Horn

7. Giblin, *The Truth About Unicorns*, pp. 67–68.
8. Quoted in Giblin, *The Truth About Unicorns*, p. 59.
9. Quoted in Shepard, *The Lore of the Unicorn*, p. 152.
10. Quoted in Giblin, *The Truth About Unicorns*, pp. 83–84.

Chapter 4: Hunting the Unicorn

11. Quoted in Nancy Hathaway, *The Unicorn*. New York: Viking, 1980, p. 131.

12. Quoted in Hathaway, *The Unicorn*, p. 129.
13. Quoted in Shepard, *The Lore of the Unicorn*, p. 199.
14. Quoted in Mystical Unicorn by Unicorn Lady, "The German Unicorn." www.unicornlady.net /legends/the_german_unicorn.html.
15. Quoted in Hathaway, *The Unicorn*, p. 134.
16. Giblin, *The Truth About Unicorns*, p. 90.

Glossary

bestiary: A book about beasts, real and imaginary. These were very popular in Middle Ages. Like Aesop, the authors pointed out lessons to be learned from the animals' behavior.

narwhal: A toothed whale that lives in Arctic Seas. The male narwhal has a long, twisted ivory tusk growing out of its jaw.

phoenix: A red and gold mythical bird said to live 500 years. Then it sets its nest (and itself) on fire. From the ashes a new phoenix is born.

plague: One of the worst epidemic diseases. In the 1300s, bubonic plague, called the Black Death, killed one quarter of the population of Europe.

Unicorn Tapestries: Seven tapestry panels that tell the story of a unicorn. Experts think they were made in Brussels, Belgium, although they do not know this for certain. In 1937, John D. Rockefeller gave them as a gift to the Cloisters Museum.

For Further Exploration

Books

Bruce Coville, *The Unicorn Treasury: Stories, Poems and Unicorn Lore*. Orlando, FL: Magic Carpet Books, 2004. The opening chapter outlines the history of unicorn lore. This is followed by a collection of stories and poems about unicorns. Many of them are by outstanding children's authors such as Madeleine L'Engle, C.S. Lewis, and Jane Yolen.

James Cross Giblin, *The Truth About Unicorns*. New York: HarperCollins, 1991. This book traces the entire history of unicorn lore. It includes a dramatic account of the unicorn hunt shown in the famous Unicorn Tapestries. Illustrations, prints, and photographs enhance the text.

Michael Hague, *Michael Hague's Magical World of Unicorns*. New York: Simon & Schuster, 1999. A collection of poetry, prose, and legends illustrated with fantastic artwork.

Jane Yolen. *Here There Be Unicorns*. San Diego: Harcourt Brace, 1994. A collection of original stories and poems by a talented author. Notes include facts and folklore about unicorns.

Web Sites

The Complete Story of Unicorns Through the Ages, The UnicornCollector (www.unicorncollector.com/legends.htm). This site contains lots of unicorn lore, including links for collecting unicorn memorabilia such as figurines, jewelry, tiles, ornaments, calendars, and toys.

Mystical Unicorn by Unicorn Lady (www.uni cornlady.net). Here you will find a wide collection of unicorn material by an enthusiastic fan of the mythical beast, including links to legends, literary references, quotations from numerous poems and stories, discussions of the evidence by the Unicorn Lady—and much more.

Unicorn Legends, All about Unicorns (www.al laboutunicorns.com/legends.php). This well-written site includes a number of unicorn legends from the ages. The site includes lots of good details.

Index

About the Author

Elizabeth Silverthorne has studied writing at the University of Texas, Bread Loaf Writer's School in Vermont, and the Institute of San Miguel de Allende in Mexico. She taught English and children's literature at North Texas State University for four years and was director of communications and modern languages at Temple College for twelve years. She has written twenty books for adults and children, as well as numerous articles and short stories. She lives in the village of Salado in the heart of Texas.